CELTIC

CHANGING FACES

PAUL LUNNEY

FONTHILL

First published 2014

Fonthill Media Limited
www.fonthillmedia.com

Copyright © Paul Lunney 2014

Paul Lunney has asserted his rights under the Copyright, Designs and
Patents Act 1988 to be identified as the Author of this work.

A CIP catalogue record for this book is available from the British Library.

ISBN 978-1-78155-082-3

Typeset in 9.5pt on 12pt Mrs Eaves Serif Narrow.
Typesetting by Fonthill Media. Printed in the UK.

Introduction

It is unknown whether or not a photograph was taken of the first Celtic team which faced Rangers in their inaugural match of that unseasonably cold Monday afternoon of 28 May 1888. If a snapshot image, as one would expect on such an historical occasion, had been caught by the camera lens, then the mists of time have erased it from view and history. Perhaps the picture was destroyed by one or other of the two big fires at the ground in 1904 or 1929, or maybe the unwanted bitter weather ruined any such idea of posing for a photograph. We will never know.

Thankfully, almost every year since the formation of these 'Bould Boys' in Glasgow's East End, a team photograph of Celtic FC has been produced. The exceptions to the rule of course being 1914-18 and 1939-45, when two world wars saw purse strings tightened and a pensive public with more on their minds than obtaining an illustration of their football favourites.

This collection contains many of those annual prints, and from the black and white Victorian early days right through to the modern era of glorious colour we can observe the many changes in football fashion and facial appearance. From the heavy jerseys, long pants and cumbersome boots of 1888 to the slick and streamlined styles of today's strips and footwear, the contrasts are certainly striking. Likewise we see how faces differ over the passing decades.

Most Celts of the early years such as Kelly, Campbell, Madden, McMahon and the Maley brothers sported moustaches. The 1930s provided us with the severe short back and sides of Peter McGonagle and Bertie Thompson, while the 1970s had Kenny Dalglish and Dixie Deans with their rock star style long hair and sideburns. The 1980s brought us a conveyor belt of bleached blond in the shape of Murdo MacLeod, Peter Grant, Maurice Johnston, Anton Rogan, Tony Shepherd and Frank McAvennie. The current crop of players are more individualistic in appearance and model a varied selection of hairstyles which range from the long lank hair of G. Samaras to the extreme skinhead favoured by Scott Brown.

Celtic: Changing Faces is a montage of team groups and player profiles from 1888 to the present day, and if the reader of this volume gets half as much pleasure as I did when collecting the material, then it will have been a worthwhile project.

Paul Lunney

May 2013

Acknowledgements

Most of the photographs in this volume come from my own personal private collection. However, due acknowledgement should be made to a number of sources. These include the following newspapers; *Glasgow Herald, Evening Times, Daily Record* and *Sunday Mail* as well as DC Thomson and Celtic FC.

Celtic 1988. Back row, left to right: J. Anderson (trainer), J. Quillan, D. Malloy, J. Glass, J. MacDonald (committee men). Second row: J. O'Hara, W. McKillop (committee men). Third row: Willie Groves, Tom Maley, Mick Dunbar. Front row: Johnny Coleman, Jimmy McLaren, James Kelly, Neil McCallum, Mick McKeown.

Celtic 1889. Players only, back row, left to right: James McLaughlin. Middle row: Johnny Madden, Johnny Coleman, Mick McKeown, Jerry Reynolds, Peter Dowds, Johnny Cunningham. Front row: Paddy Gallagher, Michael Dunbar, James Kelly, Willie Groves.

Celtic side of 1889 in London to play Corinthians.

'Darlin' Willie' Groves, Celts ace forward in the infant years of the club. His bewildering dribbles devastated defences and delighted spectators. In 1893, he became the first £100 signing in the history of Association Football when he moved from West Bromwich Albion to Aston Villa. He died of tuberculosis in February 1908, at the early age of thirty-eight.

Possil lad Johnny Campbell provided excellent service for Celtic in the 1890s. A wonderful forward, he represented Scotland on a dozen occasions, and also won League Championship medals with both Aston Villa and Third Lanark.

Celtic team, 1890-1. Left to right, back row: Mick Dunbar, Joe Anderson (trainer), Gerry Reynolds, J. Boyle, J. Bell, Mick McKeown, John O'Hara (committeeman), James Kelly. Centre row: P. Gallagher (linesman), Frank Dolan, J. McGhee, Willie Maley, Tom E. Maley. Front row: Johnny Madden, John Coleman, Peter Dowds, Sandy McMahan, Johnny Campbell.

Celtic heads and shoulders of 1891.

Celtic 1893-94. Back row, left to right: John Curran, Dan McArthur, Jimmy Blessington, Joe Cullen, Tommy Bonnar (trainer), Tom Dunbar, Johnny Campbell, Jerry Reynolds, Paddy Gallagher. Middle row: Joe Cassidy, Johnny Madden, James Kelly, Dan Doyle, Willie Maley. Front row: Johnny Divers, Sandy McMahon, Charlie McEleny.

Celtic 1895-96 photographed with the Glasgow Cup.

Celtic League Champions 1895-96.

Celtic 1896-97.

Celtic League Champions 1897-98.

Dan Doyle, Celts irrepressible left-back of the 1890s. A maverick and a star personality, Doyle was a law unto himself on and off the football field. This tall, handsome, curly-haired athlete captained both Celtic and Scotland, and could also play any sport with a high degree of success.

The Celtic team line-up for a big match in 1898.

Celtic 1898-99.

Dan McArthur, Celts brilliant goalkeeper of the 1890s, and the club's smallest at little over 5ft 6 inches tall. Wee Dan's bravery between the posts saw him frequently injured. A steel dresser by trade, he represented Scotland on three occasions and made a further four appearances for the Scottish League.

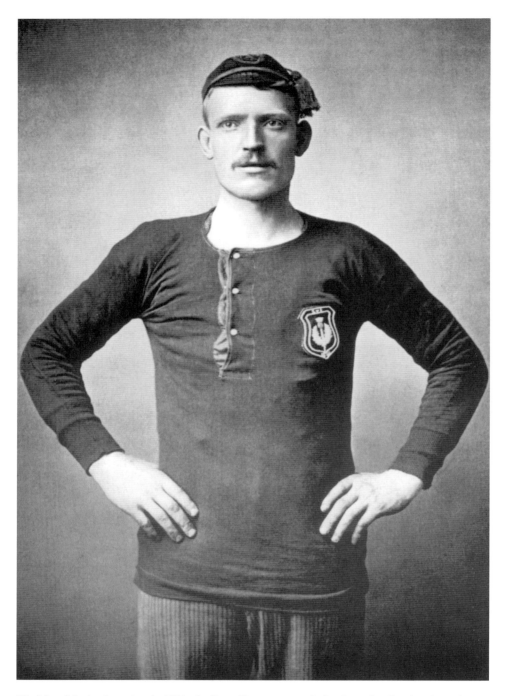

Big blond-haired centre-half Davie Russell was capped six times by Scotland, and won both League Championship and Cup. He won medals with all three of his professional clubs; Preston North End, Heart of Midlothian and Celtic. After football he worked as a miner at Fauldhouse.

Scottish Cup Winners 1899.

Celtic 1899-1900. On display are the club's honours of the previous season; Glasgow League Championship Flag, Scottish Cup and Charity Cup.

Dundee v. Celtic.

A skillful forward with a powerful shot, Johnny Divers scored in his only international appearance for Scotland, against Wales on 23 March 1895. He also starred for Everton and Hibernian, and was a member of the last Hibs side to lift the Scottish Cup in 1902. A musically inclined man.

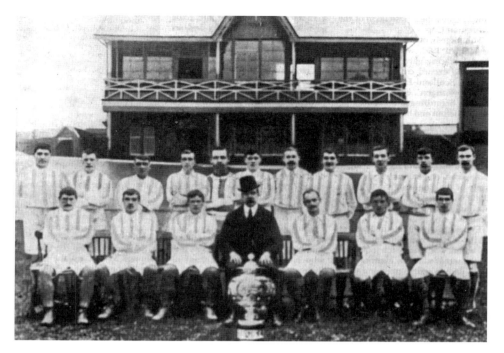

Celtic 1902. Back row, left to right: Battles, Loney, Marshall, Moir, McMahon, Watson, Campbell, Orr, McPherson, McLeod, Somers. Front row: Quinn, McMenemy, McCafferty, Maley, Crawford, McDermott, Hamilton.

Celtic team pictured at Mossett Park before their friendly fixture with Forres Mechanics on 14 May 1906. Back row, left to right: Hamilton, McLeod, Bennett, Quinn, Loney, McNair, Hay, Wilson, Craig, unknown. Middle row: Young, Bauchop, Goudie, Maley, Watson, Adams, McMenemy. Front row: Somers, Garry.

Celtic 1905-06. Back row, left to right: R. Davis (trainer), R. Campbell, D. McLeod, H. Watson, D. Hamilton, A. McNair, A. Wilson, E. Garry, J. McCourt, D. Adams. Front row: J. Young, J. Hay, A. Bennett, J. McMenemy, W. Loney, J. Quinn, P. Somers, W. McNair.

Celtic line-up in Leipzig in 1906. Left to right: Garry, McLeod, McNair, Quinn, Somers, Adams, Maley, Young, Hay, Bauchop, Hamilton, Templeton.

Celtic 1906-07. Back row, left to right: Bennett, McNair, McLeod, Young, Adams, Orr, Templeton, Hay, Davis (trainer). Front row: Hamilton, McMenemy, Somers, Craig, Bauchop, Loney, Quinn, Wilson, Garry.

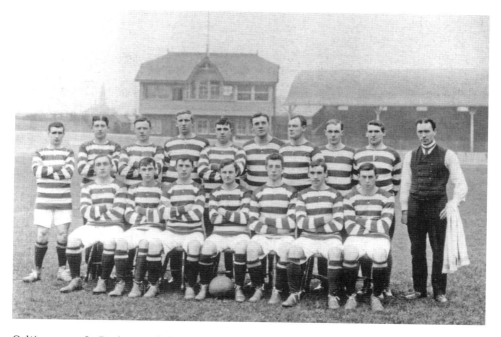

Celtic 1907-08. Back row, left to right: Hamilton, Templeton, Loney, Young, McLeod, Adams, Somers, McNair, Quinn, Davis (trainer). Front row: Hay, Craig, McLean, Bennett, Mitchell, McMenemy, Weir.

JAMES WEIR, CELTIC F.C., GLASGOW.

Described as 'strong, truculent and fearless', James Weir replaced Willie Orr at left-back in 1907-08 season. He made over 100 competitive appearances for Celtic before a dispute with the club over terms led to him joining Middlesbrough in 1910. As befitted an Ayrshireman, he was noted for his ability to recite Robert Burn's *Tam O'Shanter*.

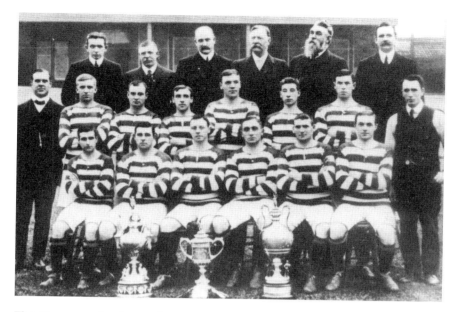

The all-conquering team of 1907-08 which achieved the grand slam clean sweep of all the honours; League Championship, Scottish Cup, Glasgow Cup and Charity Cup.

D. Adams, W. Loney, J. Hay, P. Somers, J. Quinn, J. M'Menemy, D. M'Leod, A. M'Nair, J. Young.
R. Craig, M. Moran, W. Semple, D. M'Lean, J. Weir, J. Mitchell, D. Munro, J. Dodds, W. Glover.
R. Sanderson, D. Hamilton.
CELTIC. Photographed by Maclure, Macdonald and Co., Glasgow.

Celtic 1908-09. Back row, left to right: D. Adams, W. Loney, J. Hay, P. Somers, J. Quinn, J. McMenemy, D. McLeod, A. McNair, J. Young. Middle row: R. Craig, M. Moran, W. Semple, D. McClean, J. Weir, J. Mitchell, D. Munro, J. Dodds, W. Glover. Front: R. Sanderson, D. Hamilton.

Back Row: D. HAMILTON. D. MUNRO. J. M'MENEMY. J. MITCHELL. W. KIVLICHAN. [Photo by Agnew & Son, Glasgow.
Middle Row: P. JOHNSTONE. JAS. YOUNG. J. HAY. P. SOMERS. J. QUINN. A. M'NAIR. D. ADAMS. JAS. MACINTOSH. R. DAVIS (Trainer.
Front Row: W. GLOVER. JOHN YOUNG. D. M'LEAN. L. M'LEAN. JAS. DODDS. W. LONEY. JAS. WEIR.

Celtic 1909-10.

1912

Scottish Cup Winners 1912. Back row: left to right: Directors – M. Dunbar, J. Shaughnessy, J. McKillop, T. Colgan. Middle row: W. Quinn (trainer), W. Loney, J. MacMenemy, J. Dodds, J. Quinn, P. Johnstone, J. Young, W. Maley (manager). Front row: J. Brown, A. McAtee, P. Travers, J. Kelley (chairman), P. Gallagher, J. Mulrooney, A. McNair.

Celtic 1912-13. Back row, left to right: W. Quinn (trainer), W. Loney, J. McMenemy, J. Dodds, J. Quinn, F. Johnstone, W. Maley (secretary). Front row: J. Brown, A. McAtee, T. McGregor, J. Young, P. Gallagher, J. Mulrooney, A. McNair.

Above left: Originally an inside-left, Peter Johnstone subsequently moved back to the centre-half position and was a mainstay of the side which won the League and Cup double in 1914. During the Great War he was killed in action at the Battle of Arras on 12 May 1917.

Above right: One of Celtic's greatest ever left-backs, Joe Dodds arrived at Parkhead from Carluke Milton Rivers in the summer of 1908. The fact that both Cowdenbeath in 1920, and Queen of the South in 1922 offered him better terms that Celtic, speaks volumes about the club's policy at that time.

Right-back Alec 'The Icicle' McNair was calm, cool and collected on the football pitch. Signed in 1904 from Stenhousemuir, he would serve Celtic for twenty-one years before becoming manager of Dundee in 1925.

Known as 'The Croy Express' Jimmy Quinn was originally an outside-left, before spearheading arguably Celtic's greatest ever forward-line; Bennett, McMenemy, Quinn, Somers and Hamilton. Quinn terrorised defences with his rampaging style of play which often resulted in injury.

Celtic 1913-14. Back row, left to right: McStay, McGregor, Dodds, Jarvis. Second row: W. Quinn (trainer), McNair, Loney, Young, Davidson, Quinn, Johnstone, W. Maley (manager). Third row: Hill, McMaster, Shaw, Cassidy, McMenemy. Front row: McAtee, Gallagher, Browning, B. Connolly.

A publicity card used by comedy artistes Lindsay & Harte for their 'Great Football Sketch, Celtic v. Rangers'. Note Lindsay & Harte take the places of McAtee and Browning on either side of Patsy Gallagher in the front row.

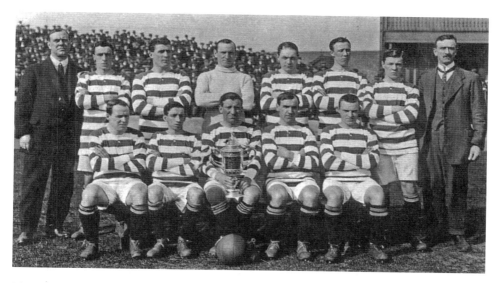

The 'Double' team of 1913-14. Captain 'Sunny Jim' Young holds the Scottish Cup after Celts recent triumph over Hibs.

Above left: Goalkeeper Charlie Shaw, along with full-backs Alec McNair and Joe Dodds, formed an impenetrable defensive triangle. He conceded only 14 goals and kept a 'clean sheet' in 26 out of 38 league fixtures in season 1913-14.

Above right: A wonderful ball-playing inside forward, 'Peerless' Patsy Gallagher is regarded by many as 'The Greatest Ever Celt'. Indeed, he was such a hero to Alex James of Arsenal and Scotland fame, that the 'Wembley Wizard' named his daughter 'Patsy' in his honour.

Celtic 1918-19. Back row, left to right: Price, Brown, McStey, Shaw, Browning, McNair, McMenemy. Front row: Cringan, McLean, Dodds, Gallagher, McColl.

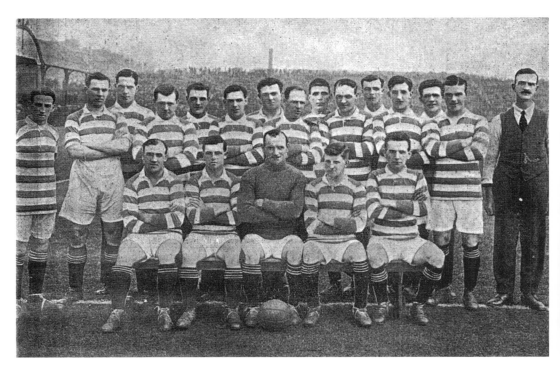

Celtic 1919-20. Back row, left to right: P. Gallagher, W. Cringan, J. Gilchrist, J. McCoil, J. Cassidy, J. Burns, W. McStey, A. McAtee, J. Dodds, A. McNair, D. Pratt, C. Watson, T. Craig, D. Livingstone (trainer). Front row: J. McMenemy, A. McLean, C. Shaw, H. Brown, T. McINally.

A strange photograph, as Rangers players Any Cunningham and Alan Morton appear in Celtic's hoops, while Celts Jimmy McMenemy and 'Jean' McFarlane pose in dark jerseys. Dating from around 1920, maybe this was a benefit match for Alec McNair.

Celtic 1920-21. Back row, left to right: W. Cringan, A. Longmuir, J. McMaster, P. Gallacher, J. McFarlane, W. McStey, J. Gilchrist. Middle row: W. Quinn (trainer), A. McNair, T. Craig, D. Livingstone, W. Lawrie, J. Murphy, J. McKay, C. Watson. Front row: D. Pratt, T. McInally, A. McAtee, H. Brown, C. Shaw, J. Price, J. Cassidy, A. McLean, W. Maley (manager).

Celtic 1921-22. Back row, left to right: J. Connor, D. Pratt, J. McKnight, C. Shaw, J. Cassidy. Middle row: W. Quinn (trainer), H. Hilley, A. McNair, J. McStay, J. Dodds, W. McStay, T. McInally, S. Glasgow, J. Gilchrist. Front row: J. MacFarlane, F. Collins, J. McMaster, A. McAtee, J. McKay, P. Gallacher, J. Murphy, A. McLean, W. Cringan, W. Maley.

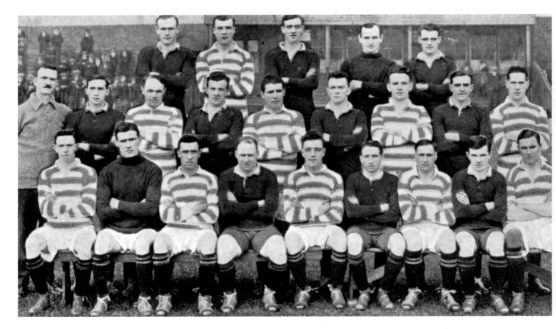

Celtic 1921-22. Back row, left to right: J. Connor, D. Pratt, J. McKnight, C. Shaw, J. Cassidy. Middle row: W. Quinn (trainer), H. Hilley, A. McNair, J. McStay, J. Dodds, W. McStay, T. McInally, S. Glasgow, J. Gilchrist. Front row: J. MacFarlane, F. Collins, J. McMaster, A. McAtee, J. McKay, P. Gallacher, J. Murphy, A. McLean, W. Cringan, W. Maley.

Celtic 1922-23. Back row, left to right: Hilley, W. McStay, Gallagher, Gilchrist, J.B. Murphy. Middle row: W. Quinn (trainer), McMaster, McNair, McFarlane, Glasgow, McLean, Cringan. Front row: McAtee, J. McStay, J.F. Murphy, Shaw, Cassidy, Crilley, Connolly.

Scottish Cup Winners 1923.

Celtic 1924-25. Back row, left to right: MacFarlane, W. McStay, Hilley, J. McStay, Thomson. Front row: Wilson, Connolly, McGrory, Gallacher, Shaw, McLean.

Scottish Cup Winners 1925.

Celtic 1925-26. Back row, left to right: E. Corrigan, A. McLean, J. McRory, J. McFarlane, V. McGrogan, D. Blair, W. Gordon. Middle row: T. McInally, E. Gilfeather, W. Fleming, P. Shevlin, D. McColgan, A. Thomson, H. Callachan. Front row: P. Wilson, W. Leitch, P. Connolly, J. McStay, W. McStay, H. Hilley, P. Gallagher, E. McGarvey (trainer).

Celtic 1925-26. Back row, left to right: Peter Wilson, Tommy McInally, 'Jean' McFarlane, Peter Shevlin, Adam McLean, Jimmy McStay. Front row: Alec Thomson, Jimmy McGrory, Willie McStay, Hugh Hilley, Paddy Connolly, Eddie McGarvey (trainer).

Celtic 1926-27. Back row, left to right: Wilson, McRory, W. McStay, J. Thomson, McMenemy, McFarlane, E, McGarvie (trainer). Front row: McInally, Connolly, A. Thomson, McLean, Donoghue, J. McStay, Hilley.

Celtic 1929-30. Back row, left to right: Geatons, Robertson, J. McStay, J. Thomson, McGonagle, Wilson. Front row: A. Thomson, Connolly, McGrory, Kavanagh, Scarff.

Celtic 1930-31. Back row, left to right: Cook, Kavanagh, Smith, Wilson. Middle row: McGonagle, Geatons, O'Hare, J. Thomson, Whitelaw, Hughes, W. Quinn (trainer). Front row: R. Thomson, A. Thomson, McGrory, J. McStay, Scarff, Napier.

Scottish Cup Winners 1931.

Celtic 1932-33.

Celtic 1932-33. Back row, left to right: McGonagle, Geatons, Kennaway, Hughes, Cameron, J. Qusklay (trainer). Front row: McGrory, Cook, R. Thomson, J. McStay, Wilson, A. Thomson, Napier.

Above left: Centre-forward Jimmy McGrory, 'The Greatest Goalscorer' in first-class professional football in the UK with 550 goals in 547 games. A powerful header of the ball, he scored so many chances with his 'golden crust' that he gained nicknames such as 'The Mermaid' and 'The Human Torpedo'.

Above right: Whether at inside or outside-left, Charlie 'Happy Fet' Napier was a handful for any defence during the 1930s. He subsequently starred for Derby County, Sheffield Wednesday and Falkirk, and collected five Scotland caps.

Celtic 1933-34. Back row, left to right: McGonagle, Wilson, Kennaway, A. Thomson, McGrory. Middle row: Crum, Buchan, Dunn, H. O'Donnell, F. O'Donnell. Front row: Hogg, Hughes, J. McStay, Geatons, Napier.

Celtic 1933-34. Back row, left to right: W. Maley (manager), A. Thomson, Hogg, Kennaway, Napier, McGrory, McGonagle, J. Qusklay (trainer). Front row: Crum, Geatons, J. McStay, Wilson, H. O'Donnell.

Celtic 1934-35. Back row, left to right: Geatons, Hogg, Kennoway, McGonagle, McDonald, Paterson. Front row: Delaney, Buchan, F. O'Donnell, Napier, H. O'Donnell.

Celtic v. Sunderland in 1936.

Above left: Skillful Malky MacDonald played in almost every outfield position for Celtic in the 1930s and 1940s. A native of South Uist, he also played for and managed Brentford, Kilmarnock and Scotland.

Above right: Long-striding forward John Divers became a regular member of the first team after Jimmy McRory's retirement in the autumn of 1937. He had an excellent partnership with Johnny Crum, which he renewed at Morton in the 1940s. His son, also John, played for Celtic in the early 1960s.

The League Champions of 1936. Back row, left to right: Geatons, Hogg, Kennaway, Morrison, Buchan, Paterson. Front row: J. McMenemy (trainer), Delaney, McGrory, Lyon, Crum, Murphy, W. Maley (manager).

A Celtic Second Eleven from the mid 1930s.

Scottish Cup Winners 1937.

The League Champions of 1938. Back row, left to right: Geatons, Hogg, Kennaway, Morrison, Paterson, Murphy. Front row: Delaney, Divers, Lyon, Carruth, Crum.

Colourful Johnny Crum was a gallus wee guy who possessed an uncanny positional sense and an intelligent football brain. As a deep lying centre-forward he developed a bewildering interchanging play piece between himself and fellow forwards Malky MacDonald and John Divers in the late 1930s.

Here's a new game. Put everyday clothes on Buchan (*above*) and Crum of Celtic, and say what they might be doing. Buchan, we should say, would look an expert skater, and Crum—well, Maryhill folks might say Johnny has struck his favourite pose in an eightsome reel.

64

Forwards Willie Buchan and Johnny Crum in full swing at Parkhead, as the 'Jungle Jims' look on in admiration.

44

The high-jump 1950s style. Chic Geatons and Jimmy McGrory hold Bertie Thomson as bare-footed George Paterson hurdles the horizontal Celt.

Empire Exhibition Trophy winners of 1938. Back row, left to right: Geatons, Hogg, Kennaway, Morrison, Crum, Paterson. Front row: Delaney, MacDonald, Lyon, Divers, Murphy.

Celtic 1946-47.

Celtic 1946-47. Back row, left to right: Matt Lynch, Dunky McMillan, Bobby Hogg, Willie Miller, Pat McDonald, Roy Milne. Front row: Jacky Jordan, Tommy Kiernan, Joe Rae, Gerry McAloon, George Hazlett.

Celtic 1948-49. Back row, left to right. Bobby Evans, Alec Boden, Pat McAuley, Willie Miller, Roy Milne, Jimmy Mallan. Front row: Jack Weir, John McPhail, Dan Lavery, Charlie Tully, Johnny Paton.

Celtic 1949-50. Back row, left to right: Jimmy McGuire, Joe Baillie, Willie Miller, Bobby Evans, Alec Boden, Pat McAuley. Front row: Bobby Collins, John McPhail, Leslie Johnston, Bertie Peacock, Charlie Tully.

Celtic 1949. Back row, left to right: Jimmy McGuire, Alec Boden, John McPhail, Pat McAuley. Wheelbarrows: Jimmy Mallan, Tommy Docherty, Jock Weir, Johnny Paton.

Scottish Cup Winners 1951. Back row, left to right: Fallon, Rollo, Hunter, Evans, Boden, Baillie. Front row: Weir, Collins, McPhail, Peacock, Tully.

Gil Heron, Celts Jamaican-born forward of the 1951-52 season. He was a man of many talents, such as photographer, singer, athlete, cricketer, poet, boxer, and of course, a more than useful footballer. He was also the father of radical folk and jazz funk singer Gil Scott-Heron.

Celts of yesteryear photocall *c.* 1951. Left to right: J. McStay, J. McMenemy, A. Thomson, R. Hogg, W. Lyon, P. Gallagher, J. McGrory. Other faces identified include J. McPhail, P. Travers, J. Delaney, W. Loney, P. Wilson. T. McInally and C. Geatons.

Trainer Alec Dowdalls shares a joke with the players in 1954.

Centre-half Jock Stein, captain of the 'double' winning team in 1953-54 season.

Celtic 1953-54. Back row, left to right: Mike Haughney, Frank Meechan, Andy Bell, Bobby Evans, Bertie Peacock. Front row: John Higgins, Willie Fernie, Jimmy Walsh, Jock Stein, Charlie Tully, Neil Mochan.

Scottish Cup Winners 1954. Back row, left to right: A. Dowdalls (trainer), Haughney, Meechan, Bonnar, Evans, Peacock, J. McGrory (manager). Front row: Higgins, Fernie, Stein, Fallon, Tully, Mochan.

As a ball-wizard, Willie Fernie's dribbling skills demoralised defences throughout Scotland in the 1950s. An Internationalist, he contributed greatly to Celtic's major trophy successes of the period.

Celtic 1954-55, photographed with the silverware of the previous campaign.

Celtic 1955-56.

BOBBY EVANS (Glasgow Celtic and Scotland), is a half-back of more than average ability. He has played for Scotland in many Internationals and his team, Celtic, has this year (1954) secured the double—top of the Scottish League Division " A " and winners of the Scottish Senior Cup.

With the heart of a lion and the lungs of a thoroughbred, Bobby Evans strode over soccer's green sward like a colossus. His aggregate of Scottish full-international (48) and inter-league (24) appearances established a record (since surpassed). He was voted Scotland's 'Player of the Year' in 1953.

Celtic players dressed in blazers and flannels on a bit of sightseeing in 1954.

Jock Stein, Bertie Peacock, Dunky Mackay and Sean Fallon play a round of golf in the late 1950s.

Celtic 1956-57. Back row, left to right: Craig, Meechan, Jack, Bonnar, Evans, Haughney, Fallon. Middle row: W. Johnstone (trainer), Goldie, Boden, Walsh, McCreadie, Auld, Mackay, McAlindon, J. McRory (manager), J. Gribben (asst. trainer). Front row: Ryan, Fernie, Collins, Peacock, W. McPhail, Tully, Mochan.

The team which destroyed Rangers 7-1 in the 1957-58 League Cup Final. Back row, left to right: John Donnelly, Bobby Evans, Sean Fallon, Dick Beattie, Billy McPhail, Willie Fernie. Front row: Jimmy McGrory (manager), Charlie Tully, Bobby Collins, Bertie Peacock, Sammy Wilson, Neil Mochan, Willie Johnstone (trainer).

Willie Fernie and Bobby Collins snowball fighting at Celtic Park in the 1950s.

Celtic 1958-59. Back row, left to right: McNeill, W. McPhail, Haffey, Evans, Beattie, Auld. Middle row: Peacock, Jackson, Fernie, Crerand, Wilson, Conway, Fallon, Mackay, Mochan, Lynch. Front row: Tully, Divers, Colrain, Carroll, Murphy, Smith, Collins.

The inimitable and irrepressible cheeky Charlie Tully, Celts 'Clown Prince of Paradise' in the 1950s.

Bertie Peacock, of Celtic and Ireland, a determined left-half, who has gained a Scottish Cup winners' medal with Celtic.

Left-half Bertie Peacock was dubbed 'The Little Ant' for his tackles and work rate during the 1958 World Cup Finals. He subsequently managed both Coleraine and Northern Ireland.

Celtic 1959-60. Back row, left to right: McNeill, Donnelly, Carroll, Fallon, Haffey, Kennedy, Mackay. Middle row: Colrain, Curran, Lochhead, Crerand, Evans, Conway, Mochan, McVittie. Front row: Smith, Divers, Jackson, Peacock, Mackle, Byrne, O'Hara.

Young Celts of 1960-61. Back row, left to right: Bob Rooney (trainer), Charlie Gallagher, John Clark, John Parks, John Cushley, Sean Fallon (coach). Front row: Billy McNeill, Paddy Crerand, Des Connor, Frank Haffey, Bobby Carroll.

Celtic 1960-61. Back row, left to right: Duncan MacKay, Jim Kennedy, Frank Haffey, Pat Crerand, Billy McNeil, John Hughes. Front row: Bobby Carroll, Steve Chalmers, Bertie Peacock, John Kelly, Neil Mochan.

Celtic Reserves 1960-61. Back row, left to right: John Curran, Jim Upton, Johnny Fallon, J. McNamee, John Kurilla, John Clark. Front row: Tommy Carmichael, Charlie Gallagher, Alec Byrne, Dan O'Hara, Jim Conway.

Centre-forward Stevie Chalmers.

Right-half, centre-half Bobby Evans.

Centre-half Billy McNeill.

Right-half Paddy Crerand.

Scottish Cup Finalists 1961. Back row, left to right: D. Mackay, J. Kennedy, F. Haffey, P. Crerand, W. McNeill, J. Clark. Front row: C. Gallagher, W. Fernie, J. Hughes, S. Chalmers, A. Byrne. Inset, R. Peacock.

Celtic Reserves 1961-62.

Celtic 1961-62. Back row, left to right: Donnelly, Kennedy, Fallon, Kurila, McNeill, Clark. Front row: Carroll, Chalmers, Hughes, Fernie, Byrne.

Celtic 1962-63. Back row, left to right: McNamee, Carroll, Veitch, Haffey, Fallon, Rooney, Byrne, Clark. Middle row: Brown, F. Brogan, Parks, O'Neill, Gallagher, Murdoch, Cushley, Jackson, Price. Front row: Rooney (trainer), Fallon (coach), Chalmers, Hughes, Mackay, McNeill, Kennedy, Divers, Crerand, Gribben (assistant trainer).

The same 1962-63 team group in colour and from a different angle.

Inside-right Paddy Turner.

Inside-left Johnny Divers.

Celtic 1964-65. Back row, left to right: Young, Gemmell, Fallon, Clark, McNeill, Kennedy.
Front: Johnstone, Murdoch, Chalmers, Gallacher, Hughes.

Celtic 1964-65. Back row, left to right: Aird, Young, McCarron, Haffey, Fallon, Brown,
Brogan, Cushley, Hoey. Middle row: Clark, Kilgannon, MacKay, Halpin, Gemmell,
McCluskey, Hughes, Spencer, Cattanach, Gillan, Kennedy, Alex Boden (assistant coach).
Front row: Jimmy McGrory (manager), Johnstone, Taylor, Murdoch, Curley, Chalmers,
Henderson, McNeill, Divers, Gallagher, O'Neill, Lennox, Quinn, Bob Rooney (trainer).

Celtic 1964-65. Back row, left to right: Young, Gemmell, Fallon, Clark, McNeill, Kennedy. Front row: Johnstone, Murdoch, Chalmers, Gallagher, Lennox.

Celtic in 1965. Back row, left to right: Young, Kennedy, Fallon, Murdoch, McNeill, Clark. Front row: Johnstone, Lennox, Chalmers, Auld, Hughes.

Scottish Cup Winners 1965. Back row, left to right: Ian Young, Tommy Gemmell, John Fallon, Bobby Murdoch, Billy McNeill, John Clark. Front row: Steve Chalmers, Charlie Gallagher, John Hughes, Bobby Lennox, Bertie Auld.

Celtic 1965-66. Back row, left to right: George Connolly, Tommy Gemmell, Ian Young, John Cushley, John Divers, Steve Chalmers, Charlie Gallacher, Jim Brogan. Centre row: Jock Stein (manager), John Hughes, Billy McNeil, Bent Martin, John Kennedy, Ronnie Simpson, John Fallon, Frank McCarron, Bobby Murdoch, Willie O'Neil, Sean Fallon (assistant manager). Front row: Bob Rooney (trainer), Jommy Johnstone, Joe McBride, Henry Quinn, Dave Cattenach, John Clark, Bertie Auld, Bobby Lennox, Neilly Mochan (coach).

Celtic 1966-67. Back row, left to right: O'Neill, McNeill, Craig, Gemmell, Simpson, Hughes, Murdoch, Clark. Front row: Johnstone, Lennox, Wallace, Chalmers, Gallagher, McBride, Auld.

'The Lisbon Lions' 1967. Back row, left to right: Jim Craig, Tommy Gemmell, Billy McNeill, Ronnie Simpson, Bobby Murdoch, John Clark. Front row: Jimmy Johnstone, Willie Wallace, Stevie Chalmers, Bertie Auld, Bobby Lennox.

When Bobby Murdoch played Celtic played. Fiorentina's coach Roberto Passaola said of him: 'Murdoch is the Papa of the team; the rest are the sons around him.' Fitting words to a man who is arguably the greatest Celt of all time.

Left-back Tommy Gemmell.

Left-half John Clark.

Inside-right Willie Wallace.

Outside-left John Hughes.

Celtic 1966-67. Players, coaching staff and Directors appear for the photograph. One suspects that they were aware that it was going to be a glorious historic season.

Celtic 1968-69. Back row, left to right: Brogan, McGrain, McBride, Cattanach, Connelly, Fallon, Simpson, Gallagher, Quinn, John Clark, Dalglish, O'Neill. Centre: Wraith, Hughes, Hay, Craig, Jack Clark, Gemmell, McKellar, Murdoch, Murray, Chalmers, Livingstone. Front row: McMahon, Johnstone, Macari, Wallace, Davidson, McNeill, Wilson, Lennox, Jim Clarke, Auld, Gorman.

Celtic 1968-69. Back row, left to right: Jim Brogan, Willie O'Neill, Jim Craig, Ronnie Simpson, John Fallon, Tommy Gemmell, Bobby Murdoch, John Clark. Front row: Jimmy Johnstone, Bobby Lennox, Willie Wallace, Billy McNeil, Steve Chalmers, Tom Callaghan, Bertie Auld, John Hughes.

Celtic 1968-69. Back row, left to right: Jim Craig, Tommy Gemmell, Willie O'Neill, Ronnie Simpson, Billy McNeil, George Connelly, John Hughes. Front row: Jommy Johnstone, Willie Wallace, Bobby Lennox, Steve Chalmers, Jim Brogan, Bertie Auld, John Clark, Bobby Murdoch.

Celtic 1969-70. Back row, left to right: Gemmell, Connelly, Fallon, Hughes, Craig, McNeill, Simpson, Callaghan, Murdoch. Front row: Johnstone, Wallace, Chalmers, Clark, Hood, Brogan, Lennox, Auld.

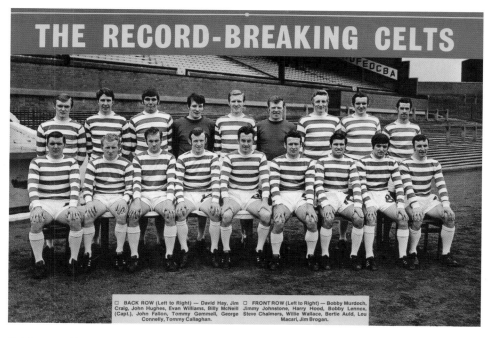

Celtic 1970 European Cup Finalists. Back row, left to right: David Hay, Jim Craig, John Hughes, Evan Williams, Billy McNeill (captain), John Fallon, Tommy Gemmell, George Connelly, Tommy Callaghan. Front row: Bobby Murdoch, Jimmy Johnstone, Harry Hood, Bobby Lennox, Steve Chalmers, Willie Wallace, Bertie Auld, Lou Macari, Jim Brogan.

Celtic 1970-71. Back row left to right: Connelly, Hay, Gemmell, Fallon, McNeill, Williams, Craig, Hughes, Callaghan. Front row: Johnstone, Lennox, Murdoch, Hood, Wallace, Auld, Macari, Brogan.

Celtic 1971-72.

Celtic 1972. Back row, left to right: Quinn, Murdoch, Callaghan, Craig, Williams, McNeill, Connaghan, Connelly, Hay, Davidson, P. McCluskey. Front row: Wilson, Johnstone, McGrain, Dalglish, Deans, Macari, Lennox, Brogan, Hood.

The same 1972 team group photographed from the opposite direction.

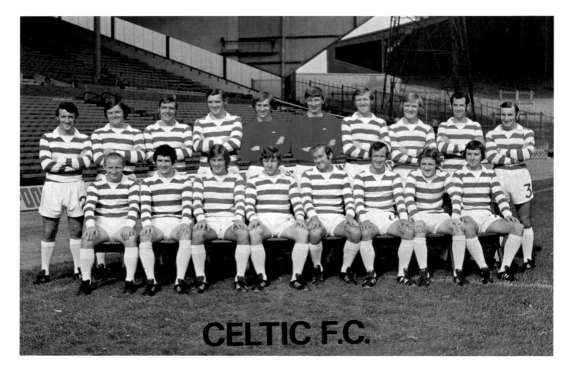

Celtic 1973-74. Back row, left to right: McGrain, P. McCluskey, Murdoch, Connelly, Hunter, Callaghan, Brogan. Front row: Johnstone, Murray, Dalglish, Deans, Hay, Lennox, McLaughlin, Lynch.

'The Double' winners of 1974. Back row, left to right: Kenny Dalglish, Harry Hood, Tommy Callaghan, Denis Connaghan, Billy McNeill, David Hay, Pat McCluskey. Front row: Jommy Johnstone, Steve Murray, Dixie Deans, Danny McGrain, Jim Brogan, Bobby Lennox.

Celtic 1975-76. Back row, left to right: Edvaldsson, Ritchie, Connelly, Hunter, Latchford, Connaghan, MacDonald, Glavin, Callaghan. Front row: Dalglish, McNamara, Hood, Wilson, Deans, McGrain, Lynch, P. McCluskey, Lennox.

Dundee v. Celtic XI in December 1975. A Testimonial Match for Bobby Wilson of Dundee. Celts line-up included players past; Gemmell, McNeill, Auld, Prentice and Hay: present; Hood and Wilson: and future; Stanton and Munro.

Celtic 1976-77. Back row, left to right: Mochan (trainer), MacDonald, Conn, Stanton, Baines, P. McCluskey, Latchford, Lynch, Aitken, Edvaldsson, Clark (coach). Front row: McParland (assistant manager), Burns, Doyle, Glavin, McGrain, Dalglish, Craig, Lennox, Wilson, Gibson, Stein (manager).

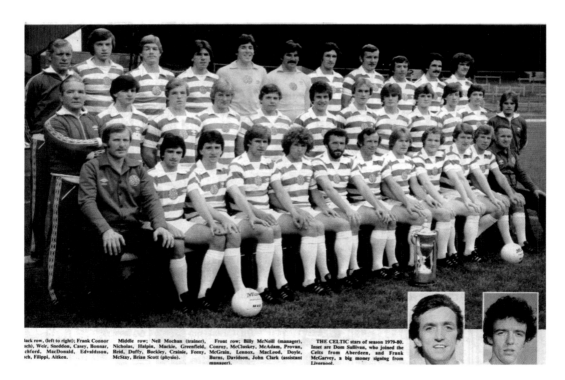

Back row, (left to right); Frank Connor (coach), Weir, Sneddon, Casey, Bonnar, Latchford, MacDonald, Edvaldsson, Lynch, Filippi, Aitken.

Middle row; Neil Mochan (trainer), Nicholas, Halpin, Mackie, Greenfield, Reid, Duffy, Buckley, Crainie, Feeny, McStay, Brian Scott (physio).

Front row; Billy McNeill (manager), Conroy, McCluskey, McAdam, Provan, McGrain, Lennox, MacLeod, Doyle, Burns, Davidson, John Clark (assistant manager).

THE CELTIC stars of season 1979-80. Inset are Dom Sullivan, who joined the Celts from Aberdeen, and Frank McGarvey, a big money signing from Liverpool.

Celtic 1979-80. Back row, left to right: Frank Connor (coach), Weir, Sneddon, Casey, Bonnar, Latchford, MacDonald, Edvaldsson, Lynch, Filippi, Aitken. Middle row: Neil Mochan (trainer), Nicholas, Halpin, Mackie, Greenfield, Reid, Duffy, Buckley, Crainie, Feeny, McStay, Brian Scott (physio). Front row: Billy McNeill (manager), Conroy, McCluskey, McAdam, Provan, McGrain, Lennox, MacLeod, Doyle, Burns, Davidson, John Clark (assistant manager).

Celtic 1980-81. Back row, left to right: McNeill (manager), McAdam, Sneddon, Aitken, Bonner, MacDonald, Latchford, G. McCluskey, Burns, Conroy, Clark (assistant manager), Scott (physio). Front row: Nicholas Sullivan, Provan, McGrain, Lennox, MacLeod, Doyle, McGarvey.

Celtic 1981-82. Back row, left to right: Nicholas Conroy, McAdam, Bonner, Garner, Latchford, Aitken, Moyes. Front row: Reid, McGarvey, Sullivan, G. McCluskey, McGrain, MacLeod, Provan, Burns.

Celtic 1983-84. Back row, left to right: Tommy Burns, Tom McAdam, Graeme Sinclair, Pat Bonnar, Peter Latchford, Roy Aitken, David Moyes, Paul McGugan. Middle row: Bobby Lennox (reserve team coach), Frank Connor (assistant manager), Sandy Fraser, James Dobbin, Willie McStay, John Buckley, John Halpin, Ronnie Coyle, James McInally, John McLindon, Lex Baillie, Brian Scott (physio), David Hay (manager). Front row: John Traynor, Mark Reid, Danny Crainie, Dave Provan, Danny McGrain, Paul McStay, Frank McGarvey, Murdo McLeod, Brian McClair, Dom Schiavone.

Celtic 1983-84. Back row, left to right: McClair, McAdam, Latchford, Burns, Reid. Middle row: Colquhoun, McGarvey, Whittaker, Aitken, Hay (manager). Front row: MacLeod, Melrose, McGrain, P. McStay.

Celtic 1984-85. Back row, left to right: Colquhoun, McAdam, Sinclair, W. McStay, Bonner, Latchford, Aitken, McInally, Halpin, Burns. Front row: Reid, Melrose, P. McStay, McGrain, McGarvey, MacLeod, Provan, McClair.

Celtic 1984-85.

Celtic 1985-86.

Celtic 1986-87.

Celtic 1986-87. Back row, left to right: McGhee, W. McStay, Whyte, Aitken, Bonner, Latchford, McInally, O'Leary, McGugan, Burns. Front row: Johnstone, Grant, McGrain, P. McStay, MacLeod, McClair, Archdeacon.

Premier Division League Champions 1987-88.

Striker Tommy Coyne.

Midfield maestro Paul McStay.

Left-back Anton Rogan and winger Joe Miller
model the club's new tracksuits.

Centre-half Paul Elliott.

Celtic 1888-89. Back row, left to right: McGhee, Stark, Baillie, McCarthy, Rogan, Whyte. Middle row: B. Scott (physio), Traynor, Burns, Rough, Bonner, Andrews, McAvennie, Archdeacon, T. Craig (assistant manager). Front row: Miller, Grant, Aitken, W. McNeill (manager), McStay, Morris, Walker.

Celtic 1989-90. Back row, left to right: Morris, Whyte, Rogan, Coyne, Dziekanowski, McCahill. Middle row: B. Scott (physio), Fulton, Stark, Andrews, Elliott, Bonner, Galloway, Burns, T. Craig (assistant manager). Front row: Elliott, Grant, McStay, W. McNeill (manager), Aitken, Walker, Miller.

Celtic 1991-92. Back row, left to right: McNally, Britton, Whyte, McCahill, McLean, Cascarino, Hayes, Hewitt, McStay, Nicholas, Walker, Galloway, T. Craig (assistant manager), J. Steel (masseur), N. Mochan (kit). Front row: R. McStay, Wdowczyk, Creaney, Grant, W. Brady (manager), Collins, Fulton, Miller, Morris.

Tennents Soccer Sixties Winners 1992. Back row, left to right: Chris Morris, Gordon Marshall, Brian O'Neil, Derek Whyte, Gerry Creaney, Tony Cascarino. Front row: Steve Fulton, Mark Donaghy, John Collins, Joe Miller.

Albanian Internationalist Rudi Vata.   Scottish Internationalist Brian O'Neil.

Celtic 1993-94. Back row, left to right: McNally, Galloway, Vata, Gillespie, Mowbray, McAvennie, Payton. Middle row: J. Jordan (assistant manager), J. Steele (masseur), Boyd, Marshall, O'Neil, Bonner, Grant, N. Mochan (kit), B. Scott (physio). Front row: Creaney, Wdowczyk, Nicholas, W. Brady (manager), McStay, Collins, Slater.

Celtic 1994-95. Back row, left to right: McNally, Boyd, Marshall, Van Hooijdonk, Bonner, O'Donnell, Gray. Middle row: B. Scott (physio), Grant, Nicholas, O'Neil, Mowbray, Falconer, Martin, Vata, W. Stark (assistant manager). Front row: McKinlay, Collins, McLaughlin, T. Burns (manager), McStay, Walker, Donnelly.

Celtic 1995.

Premier Division League Champions 1997-98. Players and staff celebrate Celtic's 2-0 victory over St Johnstone on the last day of the season.

Celtic 1999-2000.

Celtic 2001. Back row, left to right: Stubbs, Johnson, Thompson, Kharine, Douglas, Gould, Moravcik, Larsson. Middle row: Mahe, Agathe, Mjallby, Healy, Valgaeren, Petrov, Vega, Sutton. Front row: Crainey, Smith, McNamara, Boyd, Lambert, Bonnes, Lennon, Petta.

Celtic 2002-03. Back row, left to right: Thompson, Hartson, Agathe, Hedman, Gould, Douglas, Balde, Mjallby, Larsson. Middle row: Healy, Guppy, Valgaeren, Sutton, Petrov, Sylla, Crainey, Laursen, McNamara. Front row: S. Walford (coach), Maloney, Lennon, Lynch, Lambert, M. O'Neill, Boyd, Fernandez, Smith, Petta, J. Robertson (assistant manager).

Celtic 2005-06.

Celtic 2006-07.

South Korean Internationalist Ki Sung Yeung.

Scottish Internationalist Scott Brown.

Celtic 2001-02. Back row, left to right: Moravcik, Balde, Agathe, Mjallby, Douglas, Sutton. Front row: Lennon, Valgaeren, Petta, Larsson, Lambert.